Over The Rainbow

easy harp arrangement

Harp arrangement by Sylvia Woods

Id Arlen

Moderately

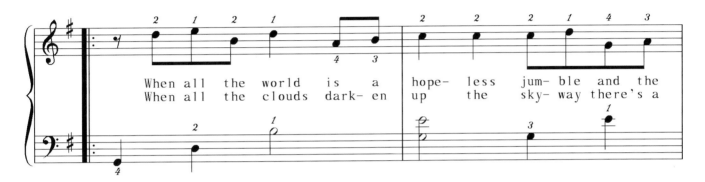

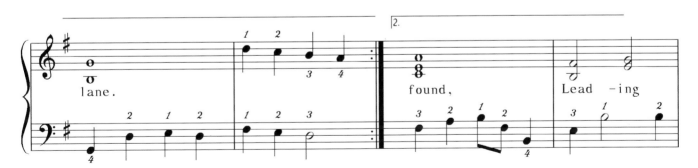

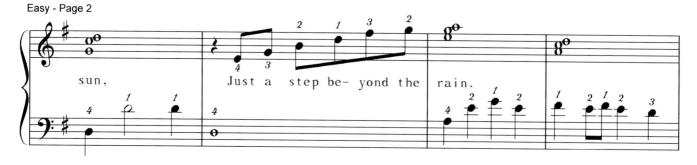

sun,　Just a step be- yond the rain.

Chorus

Some - where　o - ver the rain-bow way　up　high,
Some - where　o - ver the rain-bow skies　are　blue,

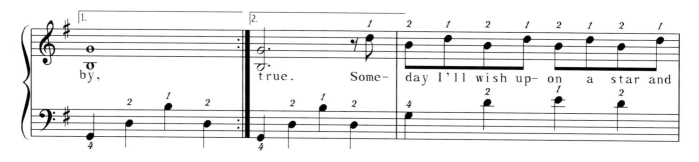

There's　a　land that I heard of once in a lull - a -
And　the　dreams that you dare to dream real-ly do come

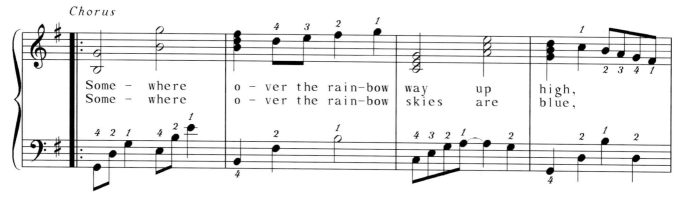

1.
by,

2.
true.　Some- day I'll wish up-on a star and

wake up where the clouds are far be- hind me.　Where

high C#

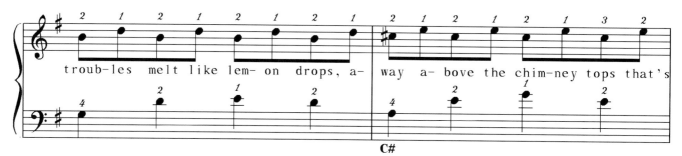

troub-les melt like lem- on drops, a- way a- bove the chim-ney tops that's

C#

where you'll find me. Some - where o - ver the rain- bow

blue birds fly, Birds fly o - ver the rain- bow,

why then, oh why can't I?

If

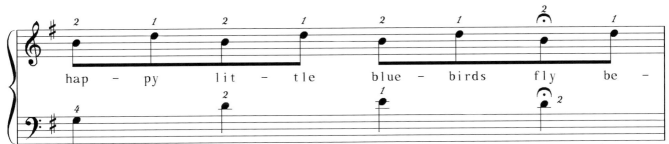

hap - py lit - tle blue - birds fly be -

yond the rain-bow why, oh why can't I? L.H. R.H.

Over The Rainbow

advanced harp arrangement

Harp arrangement by Sylvia Woods

Lyrics by E.Y. Harburg, Music by Harold Arlen

Moderately

When all the world is a hope- less jum- ble and the
When all the clouds dark- en up the sky- way there's a

rain- drops tum- ble all a round. Heav- en o- pens a mag- ic
rain- bow high- way to be

lane. found, Lead - ing
mid. D#

from your win- dow pane. To a place be- hind the
middle D♮

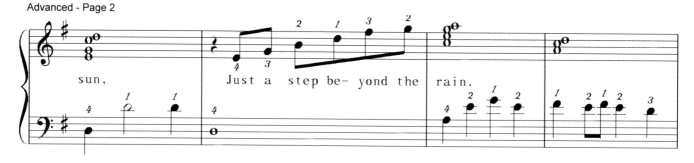

sun, Just a step be- yond the rain.

Chorus

Some - where o – ver the rain-bow way up high,
Some - where o – ver the rain-bow skies are blue,

There's a land that I heard of once in a lull - a -
And the dreams that you dare to dream real-ly do come

mid. D#   mid D♮

D#   D♮

by, true. Some- day I'll wish up- on a star and

wake up where the clouds are far be- hind me. Where

high C#

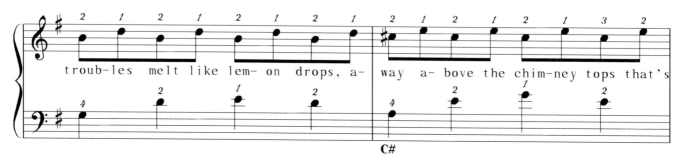

troub-les melt like lem- on drops, a- way a- bove the chim-ney tops that's

C#

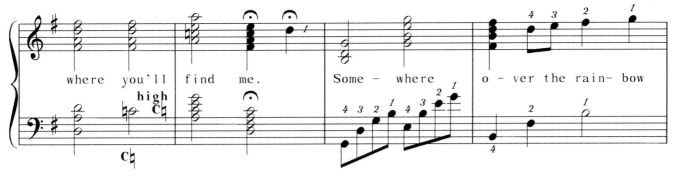

where you'll find me.   Some - where   o - ver the rain- bow

high

blue   birds   fly,   Birds fly   o - ver the rain- bow,

mid.
D#

why then, oh   why can't   I?

middle D♮

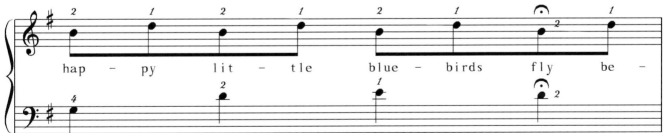

hap - py   lit - tle   blue - birds   fly   be -

yond the rain-bow why, oh why can't I?   L.H.   R.H.

Other Harp Arrangements of Pop Music
by Sylvia Woods

BOOKS:

Beauty and the Beast

John Denver Love Songs

76 Disney Songs for the Harp

Groovy Songs of the 60s

Lennon and McCartney

22 Romantic Songs

Andrew Lloyd Webber Music

The Wizard of Oz

SHEET MUSIC:

Dead Poets Society

House at Pooh Corner / Return to Pooh Corner

Into the West from The Lord of the Rings

My Heart Will Go On from Titanic

River Flows in You

Stairway to Heaven

Available from harp music retailers and www.harpcenter.com